Tangram Puzzles

Describing and Comparing Attributes of Plane Geometric Shapes

Colleen Adams

PowerMath™

The Rosen Publishing Group's
PowerKids Press™
New York

Published in 2004 by The Rosen Publishing Group, Inc.
29 East 21st Street, New York, NY 10010

1/2005 JFund $16

Copyright © 2004 by The Rosen Publishing Group, Inc.

Book Design: Haley Wilson

Photo Credits: p. 6 © Burstein Collection/Corbis; p. 9 © Bettmann/Corbis; p. 17 © Ed Quinn/Corbis.

Library of Congress Cataloging-in-Publication Data

Adams, Colleen.
  Tangram puzzles : describing and comparing attributes of plane geometric shapes / Colleen Adams.
       v. cm. — (PowerMath)
Includes index.
Contents: What are tangram puzzles? — The history of tangram puzzles — Early tangram puzzles — Sam Loyd — A tangram craze — Kinds of tangrams — Playing with tangrams — Tangram designs — How to make a tangram puzzle —A popular game.
  ISBN 0-8239-8976-3 (lib. bdg.)
  ISBN 0-8239-8921-6 (pbk.)
  6-pack ISBN: 0-8239-7449-9
  1. Tangrams—Juvenile literature. [1. Tangrams. 2. Puzzles.] I. Title. II. Series.
  GV1507.T3A33 2004
  793.73—dc21

                          2003003804

Manufactured in the United States of America

Contents

A tangram puzzle is made up of 7 **geometric** shapes. These shapes include 2 small triangles, 1 medium-sized triangle, 2 large triangles, a **parallelogram**, and a square. The goal in completing a tangram puzzle is to rearrange all 7 pieces, or tans, to make shapes of animals, people, or objects. The tans can be moved around by flipping, turning, or **rotating** them until they form a certain **design**. You can follow a pattern for making a design or make up your own.

There are only a few rules to follow when working on a tangram puzzle. The first rule is that all 7 tans must be used. The second rule is that tans must touch each other but not overlap.

Look for the square
and parallelogram
tans in the puzzle.
Both have 4 sides.
In fact, a square is
a special kind of
parallelogram. A
parallelogram has
2 pairs of opposite
sides that are parallel
and equal in length.

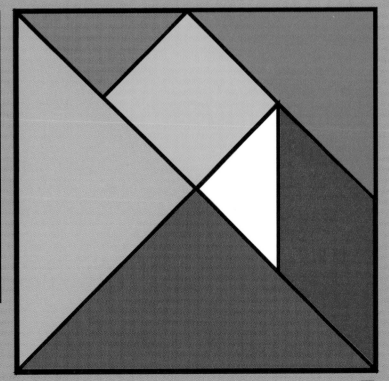

晉武帝司馬炎

Because "tang" is the first part of the word "tangram," some people believe that tangram puzzles are named for the Tang dynasty. This painting shows the emperors of the Tang dynasty.

No one knows for sure when tangrams were first used, but many stories have been told about them. One idea is that tangram puzzles were created during the Tang **dynasty**, which ruled ancient China from 618 A.D. to 907 A.D.

Another story is that tangrams were invented by a man named Tan when he dropped a tile and broke it into 7 pieces. His efforts to put the pieces back together into a square shape gave him the idea for the tangram puzzle.

Many people also believe that the word "tangram" may have been taken from the English word "trangam," which means "puzzle" or "trinket."

Some people believe that tangrams are named after the Tanka people who lived in southern China and Hong Kong. The Tanka people may have introduced the tangram puzzles to visiting sailors and traders in the late 1700s. The sailors and traders brought tangram puzzles back to America and Europe in the early 1800s.

A booklet on a Japanese form of tangrams appeared in 1742, and in 1780 a Japanese artist made a picture that showed a form of tangram. A book of tangram patterns was published in China in 1813, but by this time the concept of tangrams was not new in Asia. Wood, clay, ivory, and jade were used to make both simple and more detailed tangram puzzles.

The first Chinese book of tangrams is believed to have been published when Emperor Chia Ching ruled China from 1796 to 1820. Many tangram patterns could be found in tables, dishes, and other items made in China in the early 1800s.

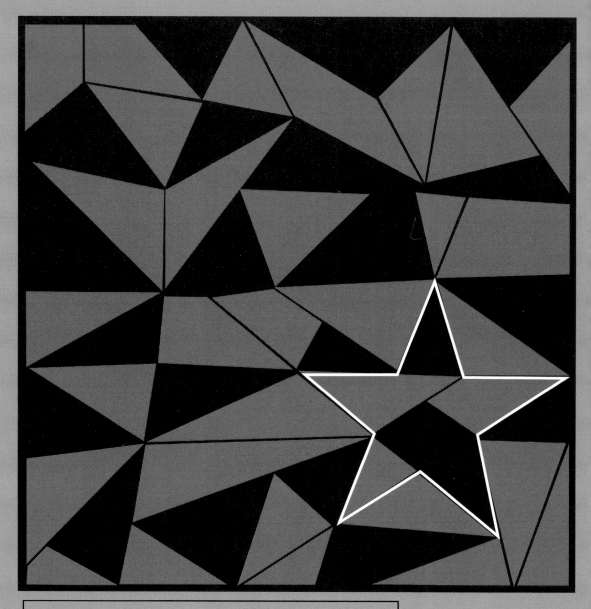

During his lifetime, Loyd produced over 10,000 puzzles. Many of them involved mathematical ideas. In this puzzle, Loyd hid a 5-pointed star among all the geometric shapes. It is outlined in white.

By 1818, tangrams were being enjoyed by people of all ages in Europe and the United States. An American puzzle inventor, Sam Loyd, published a history of tangrams in 1903 called *The Eighth Book of Tan*. According to Loyd's story, tangrams were invented over 4,000 years ago in China by a god named Tan. Loyd's story convinced many people that 7 books of tangrams had been written long before his book. Loyd also included more than 600 tangram puzzle patterns in his book. It was later discovered that Loyd's story about how tangrams were invented was not true.

In the 1890s, a German toy company produced a set of stone tangram puzzles called the "Head Cracker." These tangram puzzles became so popular that many new designs were made for people to buy and enjoy. Each set came with a booklet that showed about 100 shapes and figures for players to make with their tangram pieces. The puzzles became a popular game for soldiers during World War I, which lasted from 1914 to 1918.

As in the 1700s in China and Japan, tangrams were still being made out of many different materials. There were even tangram candy dishes made of fine china. Today, some people even make tangram puzzles out of cookie dough!

Make your own tangram cookies! Take ready-to-use sugar cookie dough and roll it out so it is about $\frac{1}{8}$ inch thick. Cut out a large square, then cut the square into the shapes you see here. Decorate with sprinkles and bake according to directions on the package.

So far we have discussed standard tangram puzzles in which only 1 set of tans is used. Another kind of tangram is called a **paradox** puzzle. Sam Loyd and a man named Henry Dudeney came up with the idea for the paradox tangram. In making a paradox, 2 designs are created out of 2 sets of tans. The designs have exactly the same outline except that 1 figure seems to have an extra piece or a missing piece.

A third type of tangram has a **convex shape**, which means there are no **indentations** along its outside edges. In 1942, **mathematicians** proved that there are only 13 possible convex tangram designs that can be made with 7 tans.

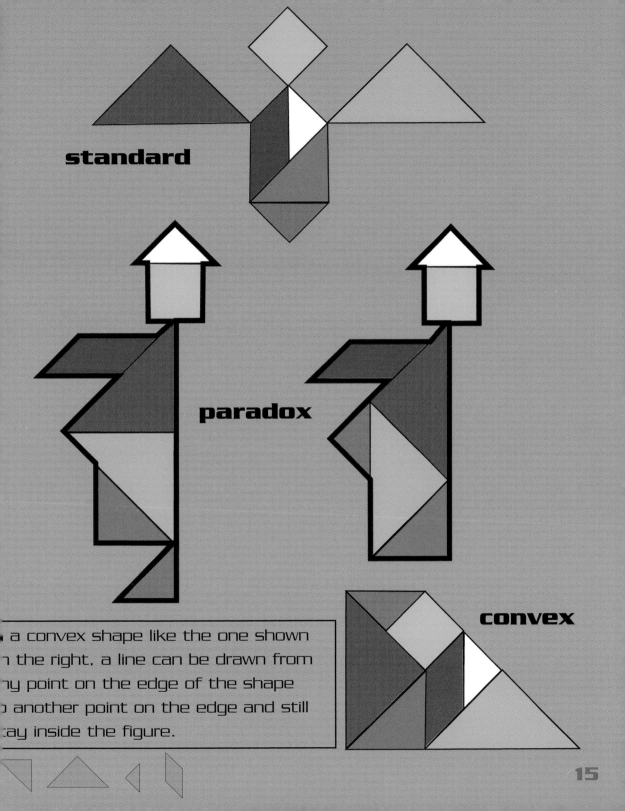

standard

paradox

convex

a convex shape like the one shown
the right, a line can be drawn from
y point on the edge of the shape
another point on the edge and still
ay inside the figure.

Tangrams are a game that can be enjoyed alone or with a partner. When you play with tangrams, you can practice by first making simple designs, then try to create more difficult designs. You can make the game of tangrams even more difficult by trying to make 2 separate shapes with only 1 set of tans. You can also try to make bigger puzzles using 2 sets of tans. Doing this makes the game more difficult because all 14 pieces must be used in the design.

When tangrams are played with a partner, each person has their own set of tans. The players choose a design and compete against one another to see who can be the first to complete the puzzle correctly.

There are hundreds of tangram designs that you can make. What other things can you make with your tans?

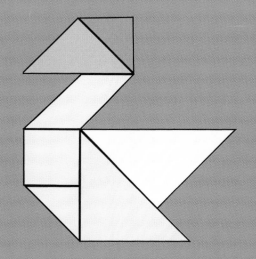

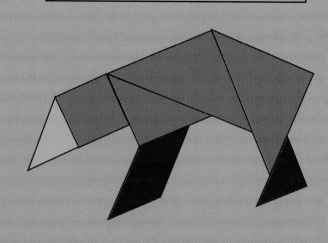

Building tangram puzzles can help us see how simple shapes can be arranged in hundreds of different ways. Some tangram puzzles show people, some show animals, and some show objects.

Look at the tangrams of people on the top of page 18. What do you think each person is doing? Look closely at how the tans are arranged to make each figure. What are the shapes, or tans, in each position? Look at the tangrams of the animals at the bottom of page 18. Can you guess which one is a bear and which one is a bird?

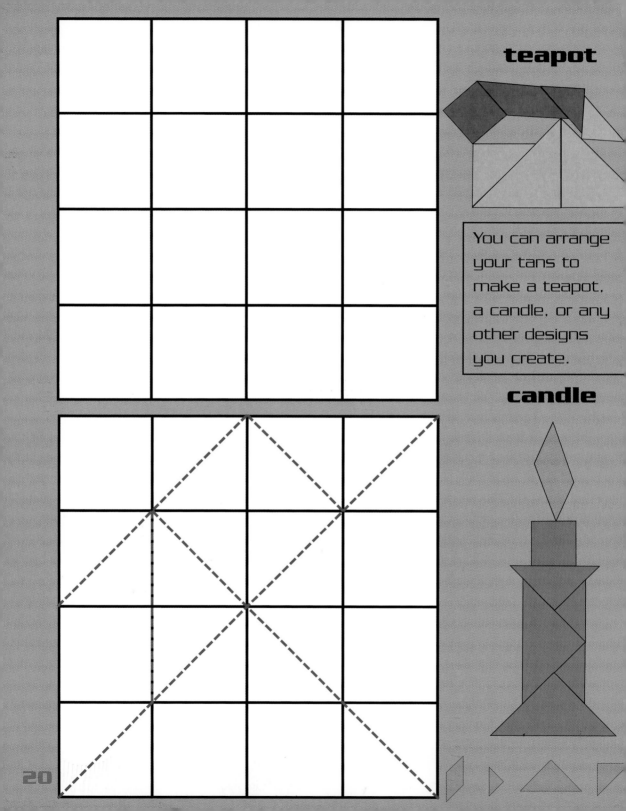

teapot

You can arrange
your tans to
make a teapot,
a candle, or any
other designs
you create.

candle

Many people make their own sets of tans from paper, cardboard, wood, or other materials. You can make your own tans by drawing a 4-inch-by-4-inch **grid** of squares like the one shown on page 20. Draw in the lines in red shown in the second square to make the 7 tan pieces. These pieces should include: 5 triangles, 1 square, and 1 parallelogram. Cut along the lines to create the pieces. Now you are ready to copy a tangram pattern or make up your own!

There are many different ideas about how long tangram puzzles have been around and where they came from. Throughout history, many people have found creative ways to solve tangram puzzles and make up their own. Famous people like John Quincy Adams, the second president of the United States, and writers like Lewis Carroll and Edgar Allan Poe were very interested in tangram puzzles. Today, people of all ages and backgrounds still enjoy tangrams as a creative way to use their time and imagination.

Glossary

convex shape (kahn-VEKS SHAYP) A type of shape that has no indentations along its outside edge.

design (dih-ZYNE) A drawing or plan that serves as a pattern from which to work.

dynasty (DIE-nuh-stee) A series of rulers who belong to the same family.

geometric (jee-uh-MEH-trik) Having to do with shapes like squares, triangles, and circles.

grid (GRID) A group of squares formed by 2 sets of lines, 1 set running up and down, and the other running left to right.

indentation (in-den-TAY-shun) A cut in the edge of something.

mathematician (math-muh-TIH-shun) A person who studies numbers, amounts, shapes, and the relationships between them.

paradox (PAIR-uh-dahks) A type of tangram that shows 2 figures that seem to be just alike, except that 1 figure seems to have an extra piece or a missing piece.

parallelogram (pair-uh-LEH-luh-gram) A flat, closed figure with 4 straight sides. Each pair of opposite sides are the same distance apart and the same length.

rotate (ROH-tate) To turn around a center.

Index

A
Adams, John Quincy, 22
America(n), 8, 11
Asia, 8

C
Carroll, Lewis, 22
China, 7, 8, 11, 12
convex shape, 14

E
Eighth Book of Tan, The, 11
Europe, 8, 11

G
geometric shapes, 4
German, 12

H
"Head Cracker," 12
Hong Kong, 8

J
Japan(ese), 8, 12

L
Loyd, Sam, 11, 14

P
paradox, 14
parallelogram, 4, 21
Poe, Edgar Allan, 22

S
square(s), 4, 21

T
Tan, 7, 11
Tang dynasty, 7
Tanka people, 8
"trangam," 7
triangle(s), 4, 21

U
United States, 11, 22

W
World War I, 12